Healing Has Come...

Keep Faith Alive!

SE SCOTT

Big Sky Publications, Ltd.
Columbia, South Carolina

This book is dedicated to every reader who has been healed because of their faith, and to every reader who is still standing in their faith...healing has come!

Healing and Faith

"See, I am doing a new thing! Now it springs up; do you not perceive it? I am making a way in the wilderness and streams in the wasteland." Isaiah 43:19

This is good news. Healing may not look like you think it should look. He is doing a NEW THING. However your healing comes, know it is from God and of God; and He does everything in perfection. He will finish the work He began in us as Philippians 1:6 says.

This selection of poems focuses mostly on mental healing for me, and my prayer is that some poem touches you in whatever area you need healing. Study the Bible for continued spiritual growth. I have included some related scriptures on healing in this book. These verses remind us of who God is in us and in the world.

He gives us a seed in our hearts, and our hands. It is a beginning, an opening, to whatever needs healing in our lives. Not just physical healing, but emotional, spiritual, and any other "al" healing.

Keep Faith Alive

Healing Has Come, Keep Faith Alive reflects what Jesus Christ died and rose for us to have. I trust that you will trust God and allow this book, Healing Has Come speak to you. You are in my prayers.
God Bless You!

SE SCOTT

Table of Contents

Healing in "I Am"

Rich
Healing Has Come
Grace
Who He Is
Qualifications
Dash Swirl
Brighter Than a Million Suns
A Prayer

Healing Love

One Who Loves God
Tell Me
No Matter How Deep
At the Cross
Found
Show Your Love
To Debbie
First, One More Thing

Keep Faith Alive

Brand New Day
It Will Be All Right

Healing Emotions, Fear & Doubt

Attitude, That Ugly Thing
This World In Which We Came
Drop Off
You Aren't A Big Bad Wolf
Feelings But Not Faith
Dead Another Day
Waiting
Deep in You
Remember
Beautiful Light

Healing Perspectives

Never Let Go of His Hand
But God
Yours to Use
All You Do
The Way You Talk

Selfie
We Who are Close
Painted Gold
Hear, Here

Healing for Courage, Focus & Strength

Pick Up Your Bed Poems
#1 All Things We Can Do
#2 Dream About Things
#3 Inside Succeed
#4 To Mimi
#5 Purpose
#6 Run Like a Garden Green
#7 Doors
#8 Who Do You Get to Be
Jewels
To the Young: Cool
Somebody's Child

Scriptural References: Healing Has Come
Acknowledges
About the Author

Keep Faith Alive

Healing in "I Am"

Rich

Rich in love; choices reign
Rich in word; free from blame
Rich in faith; unafraid of living
Nobly rich; forever giving
Always looking to meet a need
Shut down lust, craving for greed

The world sometimes is big and small
Think of others crippled by a fall
Embrace the helpless; be a generous soul
With God it is possible to live that role

Rich we are; His spirit speaks
He is the One to follow and seek
In a crowded city or rural, all alone
Wisdom draws those who are His very own
A woman at a well yearned something more
Living Water knocked at this pariah's door
In our humanity He humbly came
No sin to mention, no crime to name

Keep Faith Alive

Renewed our nature now freedom our gain
Titans die like all the same

As a flower blooms beauty in spring
Sadly falls after it brings
Briefest joy while it lasts
Long in memory before being cast
Cascading from its royal prime
Purest things succumb to time
The life of all God commands
Creative power in His very hands
Hurling down on us they land
Lord Almighty forever stands

We are rich; what remains
Of our profits our worldly gains
It is plunder left behind
Stored up bundles not yours or mine
With all striving; what abounds
His spirit holy, faithful, prof

Healing Has Come

There is no emptiness only full
Nitty gritty rawness reach, snatch, pull
God does what He says
Like water running free
Abandon all pretense in Him just be

Amazed at Almighty God is on our side
Who else goes beyond, digging deep, wide
While others bring hype unnecessary words
A barrage of nonsense
Have they never heard?
How Moses saw a burning bush
a mysterious sign revealed
He did bow humbly he did kneel
Greatness alive in Everlasting I AM
Sealed for purpose hidden in the Lamb
Searching outside, the hollowest pursuit
From the True Vine only comes healing fruit
Thoughts at a distance
On the other side of town

Keep Faith Alive

Father knows the path
Before we make the rounds

Christ did the sacrifice
For us He made a pitch
The eye, flesh, pride of life
Leads to a ditch
Dilemmas escalate, struggle, imminent fights
Revelation brings peace, focus on the Light
No one can hinder, or ever consume
The grace of God's love forever makes room
Every day, every night
Seek the One who never changes

Beware of distractions
Use of magic to rearrange us
The enemy conceals always ready for attack
Sometimes showing up in a place called lack
But those strategies deflate
Yes! Defeated and doomed, they fail
Healing has come
Jesus Christ took those nails
pierced in His hands holy and feet

Dear One
Remember the commission He gave
It takes daily courage even Moses was afraid
Tell pharaohs today Jesus Christ still saves

Conquers any power or authority we may meet
Sneak away often His face solemnly seek
For comfort, so precious, a presence perfectly complete
Healing has come
Stay there, stay there

Keep Faith Alive

Grace

Looking at rooftops that hide distant views
Here I am so far removed
From where I have been wandering
This mind of mine tries to lead
Where thoughts think they dominate
Battles from heart to head
Nothing is what it seems,
Nothing like those caterpillars following
Each other nowhere around nowhere

More than I see transforms me
Age changes, changes make changers charge
This is no game
Life grows more complicated

But I play
Learning to manage all that is outside in
Wisdom settles
A dusty house
Sense makes nonsense sometimes
Perception travels down the wrong road,

Reload one thing:
Not here on my own
I am known
By One Who is the same
Has many names
His grace is sufficient

Keep Faith Alive

Who He Is

He knows who He is—the God of Israel
First last present future and past
He knows who He is—do you?

Messed up I was so bad had
Deflated emotions, a notion to quit
Was really feeling it
Strong, like a player who could not hit

He nurtured my nature
As I read His word
It fortified the weakness
Builds up for life's tests
Wisdom to generations
Come from the Rock
The Rock of salvation
Yes He is the One who rescues
Pray for family break through

He knows who He is, do you?
Rise up, unafraid
God is mighty to save

Qualifications

Calmly, He calls the names
There is no need for particular shame
But an enemy seeks to infect me
Mosquito germs I cannot see
Telling stories about another me,
Who am I in this physical world?
More than all I see

Nerves get my best
Seems a kind of test
Do not further sink
Keep your blink. Stare straight
Control thoughts
Do not let words roll like bowling balls

How does this work; this qualifying thing
Is it so hard to succeed?
When God supplies every need, even sparrows
He feeds

Keep Faith Alive

My destiny already complete
Discovered before a frame called "me" came
I appeared before "Let there be light..." was eared

Reserved, not underserved just as I am
Nothing about me says "BAM!"
His grace can erase the reddest sin
Showing the root, from a tree within
Rising up as the righteousness of God
He is the tip and the ice burg
Every point around
Creator of space, matter, and sound
He formed me from dust and ground
No one can hold what He will unfold
Must I go on with qualifications?

Dash Swirl

A bunch of flesh standing; not him glorified
He only listens, obeys his Guide
Our ears opened; he becomes a blurb
Planting seed, preaching word
He meticulously drops a hefty bunch
Packing power words
Booming all around
Every section seized
Surrounded by sound
Brother makes points, a conspicuous hit
Chairs empty, motivation can't sit

He speaks, we ask: What did he say?
His mouth an instrument God skillfully plays
Word propels higher, a boost
He is for me; I am crazy loosed
No better place for us to be

Praising
Joyfully excited just being here
Speakers gather from far and near

Keep Faith Alive

Worshippers devour biblical meat
Feed the world, community and streets
Mark your spots--dash swirl
Ambassadors we are God's lady pearls

Brighter Than a Million Suns

God fought for me
Out, I was not
Though conditions were hectic, strained
I am still here; I remain
He—alone reigns

No cesspool pulled me down
Built-in courage lasts
Grace would not let me drown
Faith in Him I cast
Cares did not sweep quickly
Or grab my feet

His plans ordained us best
No weapon formed succeeds
In Him—we live, move, breathe
God will fight for you
Who said you were through
A liar's mouth takes blame
Never, such a thing proclaim

Keep Faith Alive

Our Father's purposeful plan
Validates you in His hand
Close your eyes see

It is only He
Who lays out a path
Savior, first and last
Forever, our God on task

Uses me even to blast
His name in frontal view
Struggle no more, will you
Just behold His light
Brighter than a million suns

A Prayer

Not to be known but to know
Christ is our life
We have forgotten the price
Our filthy rags could not pay
In love with us still He stays

Stuff pulling us away
Temporary flaky things
When God is that special someone
To have our hearts to hold
To marry live out our goals
With...
But Him we do not see
In a time of "all about me"
Forgive us of our selfish ways
It is only You deserving of praise
Not the idols we lift up or raise
As if You do not exist

Keep Faith Alive

The cost of one soul lost
Without our Savior to rescue
God is the best in me and you

This living, what is it about
Some search entertaining doubt
When Christ is our hope of glory
Settle and learn His story

Jehovah still stands strong
To Him we run when wronged
In mess, chaos or stressed
We do not remember how
When we called an answer came
God was the God we named

He has always been our rest
Peace in the mist of storm
Oh Father, help us desire You, Again

Healing Love

Keep Faith Alive

One Who Loves God

Totally invested in the Word
The rebellious ones we last heard
Absolutely, they are absurd
Do not care what the world says
Christ is the way.

Who else delivers from toils and strife?
Who else is a Keeper in this life?
Who else saves with a righteous right hand?
Who else loves more than God in command?

When I think of what He has done
That cross shows the winner and the won
New life breathes, spreads world wide
Applause to Him on the winning side
He is able

Call me fanatical!
Do not need collateral
Just as I am
One who loves God

Tell Me

Speaker One
Tell me what He said
I want to grow before I die
Tell me about temptations
This world I would defy
Tell me what He said
Please sister-friend

Speaker Two
I will tell you how
You can begin
He said to the chaos
Let there be light
On the flip side of that
He spoke up the night

Speaker One
Tell me what He said
When others lie to you
Tell me what He said
So I know what to do

Keep Faith Alive

Speaker Two
He hates a lying tongue
Deal truly for his delight
Guard your heart with care
His path will lead to right

Speaker One
Tell me on a mountain
For valleys where I weep
Tell me how to handle
Nights when I cannot sleep

Speaker Two
You are not alone
He keeps in perfect peace
A mind that is stayed on him

Speaker One
Tell me how his love towards me is true
Tell me for those times
I do not know what to do
Tell me how he died for a sinner like me
Tell me, please do, about eternity

Speaker Two
The Lord your God is with you,
Mighty He is to save
All who confess the Son He loving gave
None will ever perish
but have eternal life
This is possible
When you believe in Christ

DO YOU BELIEVE?

Keep Faith Alive

No Matter How Deep

Crimson red disappears
Maker and breaker in me
Cleanse all wrong You see
Like freshly fallen snow
Sin no more, I know
No matter how deep
That stain erased
Forgiveness takes its place
A new blameless, shameless soul
Running this race
Believing the Redeemer gives
Life in Him eternally

At the Cross

That trial that challenge that test
God used it for your best
You had courage to endure
Doubt set in making you unsure
The only thing that kept you in peace
Your courage, faith in Immanuel
It pleased Him for you to dwell
In that love you surely embraced
At the cross

Keep Faith Alive

Found

Let them frolic; let them play
I bask in Love today

I sing for joy
Read holy word
The best good news
I have ever heard

Through the thick in the thin
Still confessing how
God has been my Way Maker

Let them ski
Down the slopes
Take flights, travel abroad
I have found a Savior
A Savior
The ever-lasting God

Show Your Love

Got to trust You when the water's high
Even when loved ones die
Earth has no sorrow
Heaven cannot heal

You called me out
You know me well
You held my hand I could tell
I do not know what might be
Through this process
You always show your love
Beauty out of ashes
Dreams are not lost
Help can be found
If I pay the cost
Show your love
Living in Your presence
Trumps any fast lane
Praise and glory
To Your holy name
Show your love

Keep Faith Alive

To Debbie:

Her struggle gone now ceased
Her spirit free of dis-ease
Though earth she did vacate
We smile for our sister partakes
Of a joyous celebration
A welcome mat was rolled
And all the stories she told
About a time and place
And people who got a taste
Of her beautiful soul
A loss but a gain
Still, we remember that name
Debbie

Our temple hand over, we must
Created of mud, just dust
Our Father in heaven calls us home
We are drawn by One we adore
To study war no more

First, One More Thing

Yesterday morning
I had a dream
Of color
A purple robe
Lynn gave me

What a gift?
That is kind
Of symbolic
A robe of righteousness
Beam me up, Lord

Kingdom first
Add all things
Of life
Afterwards

Keep Faith Alive

Brand New Day

No matter how good we are or try to be
Our nature inside challenges our freedom
But holy God sent his Son
Savior, Judge, the crucified One
Who frees all bars none who come
Open your mouth; call His name
Jesus Christ there is no shame

He paid the penalty for sins
Yes we will live again
No need to try
God justifies you
His promises believe
Like Abraham did
We have rights as spiritual kids
An exchange was made on Calvary
He took our place, you and me

That robe of righteousness put it on
Feels so good to be forgiven, reborn
There was no exit after the first birth

Adam sinned for all seed
One bite he took listening to Eve
But this is a brand new day
We can confess
Christ's holy way, truth and life

Keep Faith Alive

It Will Be All Right

Getting through then to get to now
What are you wondering about, how?
To take each day like a grain of sand
Do whatever comes first to your hand
Get God's word inside of you

Obstacles will come like day and night
Keep your focus upon the Light
Know in your heart
It will be all right
It will be all right

Healing Emotions, Fear & Doubt

Keep Faith Alive

Attitude, That Ugly Thing

Verbalized bullets, a lashing tongue
Where in the world did it come from?
Some tender heart has just been stung
By attitude, that ugly thing
Needs a salve, the grace He brings

Indifferent thoughts, a don't care stance
Thinking in a way so no one has a chance
Communicating with you
Blame it on ignorance
Perhaps youth
Are you just being stupid?
Tell us the truth

Love will not let you alone
God shows mercy from here
To His throne
From here to His throne

This World in Which We Came

There is a God of Justice on the throne
He judges all on earth and will be known
He will be known
Guidelines show clearly what is right
Even oceans have boundaries
That stop in their tracks
A conscious heart prompts
Where there is lack,
Intentional choices,
Decisions that we make
Motives subtle
But truth brings light
This world in which we came

Keep Faith Alive

Drop Off

You do not know me now
Knew me back then
That was when
I did not know my place
In God to grow
Now, I know

Got to cut you short
Because that t-shirt I bought
Dirty
Got to drop you off like laundry
Who can be what God called
with negativity on their side

You Aren't a Big Bad Wolf

Called you out just today trying to whisper
in my ear
That's where you got to stop! Talk to the hand.
Your word stops.
God's word begins galloping, galloping
Eating up negative thought streams
You talk to the hand. See, you aren't
 a big bad wolf
Talk, talk, talk is all you do
On my knees I talk to you know who
Jesus Christ gives a bold breakthrough
His inoculation makes you run
There is nowhere to hide
From the power of the Son
This Christ girl is not afraid of you
You aren't a big bad wolf.

Keep Faith Alive

Feelings but not Faith

I am not alone or by myself
Somewhere, someone feels as I do
That is why I am not alone
It just feels that way
How authentic are feelings
Crooks, I say!
Just like weather ever changing
Coming, going, unsteadily
Like love turned off or on.
But, what are feelings without thoughts
And thoughts without action
Thoughts are things running through my head
If I lack what it takes, thoughts are dead!

Feeling too uneasy, shy today
Touch!
Is it not a salve that soothes
Holy Spirit, allow me to touch
Your sacred spirit within

Run away from outside things
Drama comes, and goes

Faith has no need for neurotic egos
Let the burning house collapse

Consuming leave the known
Insatiable parts of "me"
Worry--hurry
Pulling fading hair

Visuals in my mind link with divine
Peace breathes on me
Feelings have no place
When Christ daily abides in me

Keep Faith Alive

Dead another Day

There are lots of things in my head
Lots of things I cannot see
Floating leisurely by—but they die
Without faith

Disinterested things never cling
Never stay, walk, and walk away
Until I claim them
Aim them and say
"You want me as I want you"

Dream that dream in morning light
Or darkness bright
It slumbers and says
"Look at me, a possibility
Real in your mind
A horse to get behind
Follow, believe me"

In a world of zombie like figures
I wake up, sup
Forgetting the astounding things

In my heart, in my head
Embrace routine instead

Dead—another day
Without faith!

Keep Faith Alive

Waiting

Anxiety, trouble, and worry
Come as if to stay
Just believe in Jesus
Put those harassers away
Be still. Who will you trust?
Even while we are waiting
Emmanuel waits with us

God is true.

He holds with a mighty hand
A very present helper
A comforter on demand

Wait in good cheer
Praise Him, His promises--He keeps
Nestle yourself securely
In the storm Jesus did sleep
Nothing can separate us
From Love genuine, deep

Deep In You

As a child you were told
God lives in you.
It is true
Now, you are a drifter when
You need rescuing again
From discomfort, a life of waste

Hey friend, stick with the sure thing
Because chasing idols or bling
Not your heart's desire
Look inside minus the crowd
Turn down those voices too loud
Increase the value of what you say
Believe in God stop saying, "No Way!"
He will provide just get away
From negative thoughts, do it today!

Hear Him whisper softly sweet
Words of love your Father is deep in you

Keep Faith Alive

Remember

Inside a turntable spins
A tune that has no name
I wish I could remember
Lyrics, tempo, or beats
Surging upon me it gains
Demanding I hum a refrain
Sit down take a front row seat
Back through the tunnel of time
My heart does entreat but
Memory cannot unwind
One single cord

Life and the issues at hand
Push onward as I disband
The need to know this song

Have you ever been in that place?
Of unknown thirst or taste
A flavor, a touch, a sound
Tarrying you around
On it goes and comes
Beating with its familiar drum

Prancing up and down
Weighing the mind like pounds

One morning on an ordinary chore
That melody washes ashore
Aha! It was you I saw
Secretly baffling me
A jingle I loved, a friend
To hum way back then
The words came slowly that day
Etching a path, my way

To me just to say:
Everything that
Everything that
Everything that has breath
Praise the Lord!

Keep Faith Alive

Beautiful Light

You are the twinkle in our eyes
We cannot trust the world but despise
Its wayward ways
Deception distracts, strong holds pull
Our hearts get broken; we may fall
But God is whispering in a still small
voice to our souls.

Behold, the Lamb takes us by the hand
We can stand in a world
With its outrageous demands
Placed on us
Walk in the beautiful light
Not swayed by words wrong but right.

In His presence there is fullness of joy
We belong to God!

Healing Perspectives

Keep Faith Alive

Never Let Go of His Hand

An offense stands, rises, explodes in our face
A temporal moment when the enemy thinks he wins
We are thrust back from a forward spin
Our hearts may burn with dignity
A fleshly monster peers through our eyes
The words, attitude, or stance
Pierce us to despise
Keeps us from holding His hand
See through the attack that thrusts us back
Vengeance is not mine, but His
Make it end because
We must never let go of His hand

God uses frustration even mess
To provide an escape, brings out our best
On our knees, we say
Father, show us the way
Because we are distracted by offense

With gratitude and praise
Thank the Sovereign One
For allowing us to learn again

In Christ we daily abide
Offenders by the wayside
Before Him we humbly stand
Forgiving like He forgave
We must never let go of his hand.

Keep Faith Alive

But God

Hoisted over my head
Hands sparsely spread
Feet cannot keep still
Better not shut your mouth
Know that rocks will cry out
If we do not show a hallelujah praise

When I think of the goodness of Jesus
All that He has done
I become undone,
Those favored benefits
To His children not misfits
Though misfits we be
In a world that does not see His glory
Lost in praise this self
Glorify no one else but God.

Yours to Use

Just the fact that I know You
How You adopted me
You are truly great, the greatest
Of the great celebrities
Sitting high I lift You up
Reaching low you fill my cup
With blessing upon blessing

I am Yours to use as You may
Let me show as well as say
You are my God
You are my God
Thank You, Father
For loving a wretch like me

Keep Faith Alive

All You Do

Be very conscious of today
Your public moment
Your life and deeds
The "Yes" or "No"
To those in need
That harvest
What is in your heart?
Is that the best in you?
Come, peek through
Come, peek through

We are reminded, a pseudo wise voice
"Don't do as I do
But as I say"
That would never be you
Who said that

The Way You Talk

The way you talk is the way you think
You think you are the only one
With problems, aches, or pains
The only one who feels the wetness of rain
Or is misunderstood

The way you talk is the way you think
Emerging out of your heart
Repeatedly repeating a same frame mind

Mornings new you start
To haggle down God's day
You never hear worshippers praise or say,
"Great is His faithfulness!"
Not the way you talk!

Keep Faith Alive

Selfie

Before time began God knew me
To know Christ is an opportunity
No dark camera captures light
Only part
He placed eternity in the heart

Moving forward, cannot remember when
This physical frame invisible then
Yet our lives connected
Our hands touched
I know not where, a secret place
They clutched
There, a purpose given, a post
One Love viewed, Immanuel, of Christ I boast
We united up front. Complete!

In this time of imperfection,
He leads toward right, and correction
That is how I know who I am
Yes! A selfie generation I will slam
They are not a true nation
Followers of Christ, worshippers in spirit

You may not want to hear it
No need to fear it--still gospel truth

In that box see a blur that blinds
Check your reality with the book divine
Like Moses saw a burning bush
Jesus is God's beloved
Do not accept the worldly things
Simply because they are shoved
In your face

Selfie, not bashing you
Just saying the trashier you
Must remember who you are
God's child, drifted afar
Superficial fragments can never replace
The real you or the Love who calls
"Come back Home!"

Keep Faith Alive

We Who are Close

We who are close are not close
We do not make the most
Of our relationships
Some things are not based on love or peace
Or being true

That is not what we are seeing
We see "us" struggle being
Manipulative
There is no window of transparency

How are we doing in that busy place
Left behind yet keeping pace
Do not interrupt
We will tell you when
Our social is over among business friends
No backing down with humility, no bend
But our positions we defend to the end

We who are close suffer the most
Absorbed in worldly affairs
Back in the day we didn't fly away
Easily we cared.

Prone to sit, ruminate a while
Tell funny stories when we were a child
Duty was evident
Like a genuine smile
That transformed a whole community.

Keep Faith Alive

Painted Gold

No one can love you, my Dear
Hear me listen please
If they do not love themselves
You can try,
Demand why
Even cry
That mountain not easily move

You must learn a hard truth
Whether old or in your youth

Turn the page; move on
God is surely for you
Do not be dismayed
That relationship will in time fade
You are totally whole
Be strong, courageously bold
Because in someone else's eyes
You are painted gold

Hear, Here

How important is God to you
Is He worth more than money?
More valuable than fill-ins,
A diamonded Honey,
That makes you go, Wow
But when do you bow
To God giving thanks

How important is God to you
His laws teach wisdom, guidance too
They keep us from losing life
Those boundaries maintain control
Like a stop prevents a crash
This world you love
It will smash the toughest soul
Do you see His eyes on you?
He is not scary but oh, so true
A part of your being is grounded to
The everlasting God deep inside,

Keep Faith Alive

Deeper still
Listen closer, hear
Here He is to cover you, only believe
Only believe

Healing for Courage, Focus & Strength

Keep Faith Alive

All Things We Can Do #1

Do not mark me in a snare
Just do your best; pull me out from there
I see a majority
Don't judge because I walk confidently
Like somebody's ambassador

You are gifted too;
Choose life in all you behold
That measuring cup is only a guide
Expand your borders far and wide
There is a limitless power inside

Recognize, the next level
I encourage you
Confess His words
For they are true
All things we can do
Through Christ who
Strengthens us

Dream about Things #2

Dream about things beyond your grasp
What can you imagine?
Where is your vast?
Mountain not too high
Valley depths try
Stretch out, leave that mold
Let God take complete control
Praise to His holy name
Dream about things beyond your grasp
Even when others tell you no
Or say it's just a common Joe
Never, ever let your dream go
It might be rough, hold on tight
Exit yourself straight to the right
Think, plan, and strategize
In time the winner claims the prize

Dream about things beyond your grasp
Approach your dream like a highly called task
Knock, seek ask too
Remember Christ gave you "things to do".

Keep Faith Alive

Inside Succeed #3

Are you for real or not as you seem
Where are your efforts, purpose and dream?
Your dream
You know what it is like?
When you can't see?
Through the shade, deepening mist

Got to keep it moving like you belong
Though the darkness is prolonged
Or you feel empty inside
Answers are there yes they hide
Who do you get to be?
Subconscious thoughts say greater is He
Inside you creativity

Are you deliberate?
Did you schedule a plan?
Too many questions
What's in your hand?

Resting inside a giant sleeps
Learn this stranger
Wake up the deep see in you
An ocean never sailed, never knew

It is not by might, power or speed
God's inside
Inside succeed.

Keep Faith Alive

To Mimi: #4

Walking along the way
Opportunity tilts his head
Are you going to buckle?
Or pick up your bed?

Think through the process
Hash it out
Discard any opening of fear or doubt
Mistakes, they will happen
Challenges will appear
Increase your effort
Mimi, do you hear
The path is paved with you in mind
Move forward believe for yourself
Don't look at others;
Stay focused on no one else
Etched in your heart
The Spirit wants to speak
Start moving upwards,
Talk to others is cheap
You can certainly do this

Purpose #5

There is a price to pay
All seeds that got through
God has a plan especially for you
He brings goodness, a future, a hope
Seasons, time, and scope
Life with a heart to reach
Lessons grand to learn or teach
Get up, Warrior
You are not dead
A battle is on
Pick up your bed
Crawl, walk, run
Know whose you are
Daughters, sons

The enemy does not reign
His warped mission is to gain
An advance on God's property
Though a loser in him we see
Some live in darkness as he
They are defeated foes

Keep Faith Alive

We glorify the Light
Make what is wrong, right
We say to you who fight
Be strong

But woe to corrupted seed

Run Like a Garden Green #6

Some dreams will never die
Though various others try
To kill them before they root
Like another target, they shoot
But dreams crushed in earth
Sprout with talent grow worth
While hidden in places unseen

From darkness comes a garden green
Touch hearts laden down
Give hope to nations to towns

Dreams that hang around
Come back like a fighter rebounds
Until duty is done
Dreamers shine like a sun
That catches their throw
Then run

Keep Faith Alive

Doors #7

When the Lord closes doors we should leave them closed
We miss blessings because we are exposed
Relaxed in that comfortable place
Get Up!
Make haste!
We don't understand
How the Man works out His plan

Sometimes, we stare so long
At doors that are shut
Disappointment sets in
Especially when
We are anxious to know
What He takes time to show
"It will not tarry"
The vision won't
Isn't that what Jesus said
Believe! Pick up your bed

Rest in Him who is never late
An on time God celebrate
That open door
You never saw before
So what,

He is right there, speaking
Walk on to a level
Bright and sparkling
That brand in you
New

Keep Faith Alive

Who Do You Get to Be #8

You get to be
A seeker
A knocker
An asker at the door
Live in Him, live even more
Nothing can truly hold you back
The Lord is Shepard
There is no lack
Who do you get to be?
Pray for guidance until you see
What perfect gifts He has in you

To the Young: Cool

When cool gets cold after you are old
Or maybe not because you got shot
Hanging with friends
No destination, no plan to begin
What dreams do you command?
Boring is what you say
Here are my questions:

Was Brooks right
In that poem was "cool" too tight
Your inactivity must be restrained
Get the other you not so lame
Where's the muscle you need to flex
Here's a worthy goal: seek the thing that's next
Be determined, your lazy fight
Take that chance to make yourself right

Cool is good but makes sense
If you are not straddling
Procrastination's fence

Be brave, be bold
Keep Faith Alive

Stop living life on hold
Stretch out, imagine you somewhere
Positive
Show that you care

A makeover, please
Do an update
Amendments accepted
It is not too late.
To be really cool

Jewels

Got credit young
An accomplishment then
Back in college a choice when
Freedom came to spend, spend, and spend
What smiles of entitlement?
Credit was great fun
A never before privilege I had won
Consequences for actions I knew no clue
Years later brought me to
A realization, a bad fall
Charge took my future and all
The money I meant to save
Left me nursing a financial grave
Exactly how a lifetime slave is born
Terrible habits we don't see at first
Until shattered lives get worse and worse
But God provides an open door
He teaches that "things" are not worth more
Than the jewels He put inside
A Savior to go to, wisdom to know who
Gets the glory and praise

Keep Faith Alive

Somebody's Child

He was just a kid we forgot
Many more after him were shot
An angel he was not
But he was somebody's child
He like others deserved to stay
To find his place and make his way
God will do justice on his day

It was a simple thing, maybe not
Time moved along as the night
Brought him to a fatal shot
Stories perceived, parents grieved

Then there was the truth

To see a child, a body laid
So unfortunately in a grave
Thoughts of some demand change
That is bound to come
Bound to come
Certainly

Scripture References for Healing Has Come

Healing in "I Am"
Exodus 15:26; Jeremiah 17:14; Romans 8:11

Healing Love
Psalm 103:1-5; Malachi 4:2; John 3:16

Healing Emotions, Fear & Doubt
Isaiah 12:2; Psalm 147:3; 3 John 2

Healing Perspectives
Psalm 73:24-26; Proverbs 4:20-22; Mark 5:34

Healing for Courage, Focus & Strength
"Pick up Your Bed" Poems
Isaiah 41:10: Philippians 4:13; I Corinthians 10:13; John 5:1-9

Keep Faith Alive

ACKNOWLEDGEMENTS

First of all I would like to thank my Father God for continuing to do a new thing in me. He is certainly a keeper, the author and finisher of my faith.
Thanks to all of those in the body of Christ who have encouraged me in writing these poems, even those I do not personally know but have heard. May God continue to use you for His purpose. Your words did not fall on deaf ears.
I am always appreciative of my loving husband who patient and encouraging. He is a great supporter and friend.

Finally, thanks to those who have read, recited, and shared my poems with others, especially young people who will always hold a special place in my heart, so many of these poems were written with you in mind. God has a special place in this world for you to make a dynamic impact.

Keep him in the forefront of your life and you will never go wrong.
We found in Him a resting place, and He has made us glad!

Keep Faith Alive

About The Author

SE Scott was born in Summerton, South Carolina. She has lived in Florida, New York, and New Jersey. She has travelled internationally.

She now resides in Columbia, South Carolina with her husband, Lynn.

Since retiring as a teacher of English for 30 years, SE has devoted much of her time to writing, media production, community activities, travel, and family.

She also lectures about writing and poetry in schools and other institutions around the country.

SE Scott is co-author of the play, A Pearl of a Girl, a coming of age story about five inner city teenage girls.

This is SE Scott's fourth published work. Her books include, Keep Smiling, Standing Strong, Got to Keep it Moving, and A Pearl of a Girl are all available on Amazon.com and in other bookstores. Some of her poems can be viewed on

YouTube under the name Mustang2lady. You can email SE at essiece@gmail.com, or listen to her talk shows, Here by DeSign and Healing Has Come on Blogtalkradio.com.

* * *

Keep Faith Alive

Notes

www.ingramcontent.com/pod-product-compliance
Lightning Source LLC
Chambersburg PA
CBHW032024040426
42448CB00006B/715